Ideas for micro users

written by TONY GRAY Cert Ed, M A
*Director of the Loughborough Primary Micro Project,
Loughborough University of Technology*

and

CARL BILLSON Cert Ed, M A, M Sc
*Loughborough Primary Micro Project,
Loughborough University of Technology*

Ladybird Books Loughborough

Playing with words

Have you read this kind of thing in comics?

"YOU WILL EACH WRITE, 'I MUST NOT EAT SWEETS IN CLASS," TWENTY TIMES

Let's imagine we are in this class! We can use a computer to help us to write these lines. Type in the following short program. Remember, *do not* press RETURN until you want to begin with a new line number.

```
10 FOR N = 1 TO 20
20 PRINT ''I must not eat sweets
in class.''
30 NEXT N
```

Using a computer, it is easy to write the same thing over and over again.

Let's look at another way of writing the same thing lots of times. Try to make your name appear in different positions until there are a hundred or more of you!

Each new position for your name will need new values for the row and column. We can use RND to select these values so that your name will appear in different positions at random.

```
10 CLS
20 FOR N=1 TO 100
30 LET xpos=INT (RND*28)
40 LET ypos=INT (RND*21)
50 PRINT AT ypos,xpos;"Steve"
60 PAUSE 10
70 NEXT N
```

```
10 CLS
20 FOR I = 1 TO 100
30 X=RND(35)
40 Y=RND(23)
50 PRINT TAB(X,Y)"STEVE";
60 wait=INKEY(100)
70 NEXT I
```

Can you alter this to include colours?

What happens if you add this line?

```
65 CLS
```

Try it and see.

Could you get two words – say CAT and MOUSE – to chase each other all over the screen? If MOUSE is at position (r,c) then CAT might appear nearby at (r + 2, c + 5).

The program below will start you off. To make them chase, press a key.

```
10 PAPER 0
20 LET xpos=INT (RND*23)
30 LET ypos=INT (RND*20)
40 CLS
50 INK 7
60 PRINT AT ypos,xpos;"mouse"
70 INK 6: PAUSE 7
80 PRINT AT ypos+1,xpos+6;"CAT
"
90 IF INKEY$="" THEN GO TO 90
100 GO TO 20
```

```
10 X=RND(30)
20 Y=RND(22)
30 CLS
40 PRINT TAB(X,Y)CHR$(131)"mouse"TAB(
X+6,Y+1)CHR$(129)"CAT"
50 ch$=GET$
60 GOTO 10
```

Word pictures

Have you ever tried writing poems that are pictures at the same time? The computer can make these word pictures come alive.

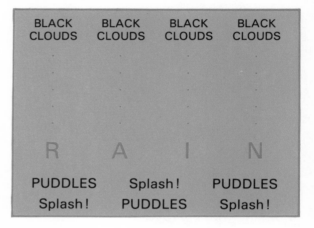

1 The BLACK CLOUDS come along.
2 The R A I N falls steadily.
3 'Splash!' The rain leaves PUDDLES.

You should be able to get the clouds and puddles printed. What about the falling rain?

THE PROGRAM OVERLEAF WILL HELP YOU

```
20 CLS
30 FOR y=0 TO 20 STEP 0.5
40 PRINT AT y,0;"  .    .
    .    ."
50 PRINT AT y+1,0;"   R      A
   I    N"
60 NEXT y
70 GO TO 20
```

```
20 CLS
30 FOR ypos=0 TO 23
40 PRINT TAB(0,ypos)"  .       .
      .     ."
50 PRINT TAB(0,ypos+1)"   R       A
       I     N"
60 FOR I=1 TO 500:NEXT
70 NEXT
80 GOTO20
```

Have a go at making the complete
story picture of a rainy day.

Other commands will change the colour
of the writing, make some words flash or
change the background colour. Try
including some of these effects in your
programs. Your computer manual will
have details.

HERE ARE SOME
EXAMPLES

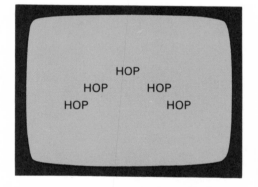

```
            SMOKESMOKE
            SMOKESMOKE

        CHIMNEY
        CHIMNEY
        CHIMNEY
        CHIMNEY
        CHIMNEY
        CHIMNEY
        ROOFROOFROOFROOFROOF
        ROORROOFROOFROOFROOF
```

```
              HOP
        HOP         HOP
    HOP                 HOP
```

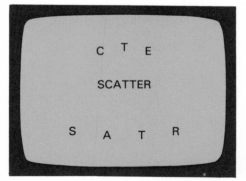

```
        C   T   E

          SCATTER


    S       A       T   R
```

4

Moving pictures

Have you seen cartoons on television?
To make the pictures move involves a process called ANIMATION.

Look at this:

```
10 PRINT AT 10,15;"-O  ,"
20 PRINT AT 11,15;"    "
```

```
10 PRINT "-O    "
20 PRINT CHR$(151)CHR$(255)CHR$(255)
   CHR$(255)
```

If you type this code into your computer it will draw a little duck when you run the program. Let's call him Sam.

It might be nice to make Sam swim across the screen!

HOW CAN I
DO THAT ?

Well what we do is this...

1 We draw some water.

2 Then we draw Sam on the water.

3 We rub Sam out and...

4 ...re-draw him in a different position.

If you do this quickly and lots of times it looks as though Sam is swimming across the screen.

See if you can work out how to do this on your computer. There's one way of doing this below.

```
20 FOR a=20 TO 0 STEP -1
30 LET d=9
40 FOR v=0 TO 25: INK 5: PRINT
AT d+2,v;"■": NEXT v
50 INK 0: PRINT AT d,a;"-O ,"
;TAB a;" ■■ "
70 NEXT a
```

```
10 CLS
20 PRINT TAB(0,19)CHR$(151)'CHR$(148)
30 FOR I=1 TO 39:PRINTCHR$(255);:NEXT
40 FOR dukpos =34 TO 1STEP-1
50 PRINT TAB(dukpos,18)"-O , ";
60 PRINT TAB(dukpos,19)"
"CHR$(255)CHR$(255)CHR$(255)" "''
65 FOR J = 1 TO 50:NEXT
70 NEXT
```

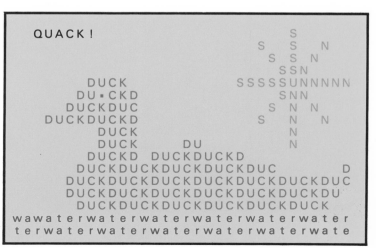

Making pictures

What about making pictures out of letters?

WHAT DO YOU MEAN?

Look at this:

This is Sam's big brother, Syd. As you can see, he is made out of letters. Depending on your computer, you might be able to make him coloured.

```
QUACK!                              S
                              S     S     N
                                S   S   N
                                 SSN
            DUCK             SSSSSUNNNNN
           DU•CKD                 SNN
          DUCKDUC              S   N   N
         DUCKDUCKD           S     N     N
           DUCK                    N
           DUCK       DU           N
          DUCKD  DUCKDUCKD
         DUCKDUCKDUCKDUCKDUC                D
        DUCKDUCKDUCKDUCKDUCKDUCKDUC
        DUCKDUCKDUCKDUCKDUCKDUCKDU
         DUCKDUCKDUCKDUCKDUCKDUCK
wawaterwaterwaterwaterwaterwater
terwaterwaterwaterwaterwaterwate
```

6

HOW IS IT DONE?

First of all you draw your picture. You could trace it from a book if you like. Simple designs are easiest at first.

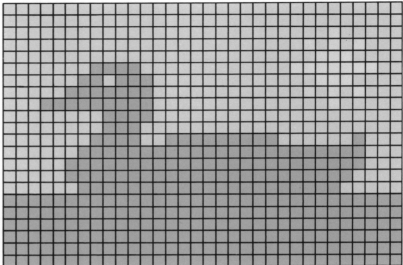

Then you draw it on squared paper, making sure that it will fit your computer's screen. The more squares you have the better the picture.

REMEMBER, Spectrum pictures can only be up to 32 × 22 because the bottom two rows of characters cannot be used for graphics. The size of BBC pictures varies with the MODE used.

Next, you write in the letters.

You need not use just one word. You could use any of the letters or punctuation marks. Syd has a full stop (.) for his eye.

Finally you turn this into a program by putting the letters into PRINT statements (see your manual.) Be sure to leave the correct number of spaces at the start of each line or the shapes in your picture won't be in the correct places.

When you run the program it will draw your duck! Try this for yourself. If you get stuck look at the program on page 8.

You can draw anything using this method. By mixing up the upper and lower case letters, punctuation marks, numbers and graphics characters you can draw pictures, maps, messages – anything!

Big duck program

```
10 PRINT TAB 26;"S"
20 PRINT "QUACK!";TAB 23;"S  S
 N"
30 PRINT TAB 24;"S S N"
40 PRINT TAB 25;"SSN"
50 PRINT TAB 7;"DUCK";TAB 21;"
SSSSSUNNNNN"
60 PRINT TAB 6;"DU.CKD";TAB 25
;"SNN"
70 PRINT TAB 5;"DUCKDUC";TAB 2
4;"S N N"
80 PRINT "   DUCKDUCKD";TAB 23
;"S N N"
90 PRINT TAB 8;"DUCK";TAB 26;"
 N"
100 PRINT TAB 8;"DUCK";TAB 16;"
DU";TAB 26;"N"
110 PRINT TAB 7;"DUCKD DUCKDUCK
D"
120 PRINT TAB 6;"DUCKDUCKDUCKDU
CKDUC     D"
130 PRINT TAB 5;"DUCKDUCKDUCKDU
CKDUCKDUCKDUC"
140 PRINT TAB 5;"DUCKDUCKDUCKDU
CKDUCKDUCKDU"
150 PRINT TAB 6;"DUCKDUCKDUCKDU
CKDUCKDUCK"
160 PRINT "wawaterwaterwaterwat
erwaterwater"
170 PRINT "terwaterwaterwaterwa
terwaterwate"
180 INK 0
```

```
10 PRINT SPC26"S"
20 PRINT " QUACK!"SPC16"S  S  N"
30 PRINT SPC24"S S N"
40 PRINT SPC25"SSN"
50 PRINT SPC7"DUCK"SPC10"SSSSSUNNNNN"
60 PRINT SPC6"DU.CKD"SPC13"SNN"
70 PRINT SPC5"DUCKDUC"SPC12"S N N"
80 PRINT "   DUCKDUCKD"SPC11"S  N  N"
90 PRINT SPC8"DUCK"SPC14"N"
100 PRINT SPC8"DUCK"SPC4"DU"SPC8"N"
110 PRINT SPC7"DUCKD DUCKDUCKD"
120 PRINT SPC6"DUCKDUCKDUCKDUC
KDUC"SPC6"D"
130 PRINT SPC5"DUCKDUCKDUCKDUCKDUCKDUC
KDUC"
140 PRINT SPC5"DUCKDUCKDUCKDUCKDUCKDUC
KDU"
150 PRINT SPC6"DUCKDUCKDUCKDUCKDUCKDUC
K"
160 PRINT "waterwaterwaterwaterwaterwa
terwa"
170 PRINT "terwaterwaterwaterwaterwate
rwate"
```

The project on page 12 shows another idea. Also, if someone in your family is interested in knitting, have a look at a pattern. You will find that pictures in knitting are made in just the same way as Syd. You could try writing a computer program to match your sweater!

Super sounds

To make sounds, the computer needs information about how long each note lasts (*duration*) and whether it is high or low (*pitch*). Each computer has its own commands to make sounds so have a look in your manual.

Here are some sounds. Try them...

```
BEEP 5,25
BEEP 1,-30
BEEP .1,0
```

```
SOUND 3,-15,201,100
SOUND 3,-15,29,20
SOUND 3,-15,101,2
```

Change the values and listen to the effects.

What about the beat or rhythm of the sounds?

The beat in music is very important. Today, many pop groups use computers to synthesise rhythms. They are called drum machines. You can turn your computer into a drum machine.

9

To get you started, here are two short programs.

```
10 GO SUB 100: GO SUB 300: GO
SUB 200: GO SUB 400: GO SUB 200:
GO SUB 400
20 GO TO 10
100 REM low note
110 BEEP .1,-5: RETURN
200 REM high note
210 BEEP .1,0: RETURN
300 REM long pause
310 PAUSE 5: RETURN
400 REM short pause
410 PAUSE 1: RETURN
```

```
10 GO SUB 100: GO SUB 300: GO
SUB 200: GO SUB 300: GO SUB 200:
GO SUB 300
20 GOTO 10
100 REM low note
110 BEEP .2,-5: RETURN
200 REM high note
210 BEEP .2,0: RETURN
300 REM pause
310 PAUSE 5: RETURN
```

```
10 PROClow:PROClong:PROChigh:PROCshor
t:PROChigh:PROCshort
20 GOTO 10
30 DEF PROClow:SOUND3,-15,81,5:ENDPRO
C
40 DEF PROChigh:SOUND3,-15,101,5:ENDP
ROC
50 DEF PROClong:FOR w=1 TO 900:NEXT:E
NDPROC
60 DEF PROCshort:FOR w=1 TO 400:NEXT:
ENDPROC
```

```
10 PROClow:PROCrest:PROChigh:PROCrest
:PROChigh:PROCrest
20 GOTO 10
30 DEF PROClow:SOUND3,-15,81,5:ENDPRO
C
40 DEF PROChigh:SOUND3,-15,101,5:ENDP
ROC
50 DEF PROCrest:FOR w=1 TO 750:NEXT:E
NDPROC
```

These programs create different rhythms from notes and pauses. Low and high notes make the beat easier to hear. This is like using a bass drum and a side drum.

The way to find other interesting rhythms is to listen to records and work out the beat, using notes and pauses. You should experiment a lot because this is the only way to get the effects you want. Some musicians take weeks to find the exact sound they want for a record.

Why not set the computer playing the rhythm and you join in on a recorder or waste-paper bin! You could form a band all on your own.

Computer projects

On the following pages there are some projects for you to try.

They're not for you to copy but are ideas to start you off creating your own programs. Don't forget you can use the information in the first part of the book to help you. To make your programs interesting, try using sound, pictures, colour, movement and words.

Don't forget to plan your program.

All programmers plan their projects very carefully. This is called *designing* the program.

They often use squared paper to help them to get the pictures and words in the right place before they start writing the program in BASIC (Beginners All-purpose Symbol Instruction Code.) They also use flow charts to make sure that things happen in the right order. Here's one...can you follow it?

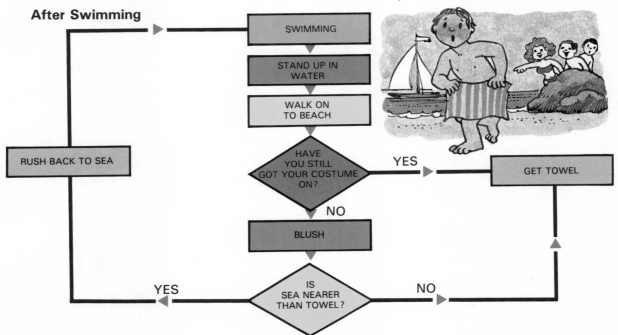

After Swimming

SWIMMING → STAND UP IN WATER → WALK ON TO BEACH → HAVE YOU STILL GOT YOUR COSTUME ON?

YES → GET TOWEL

NO → BLUSH → IS SEA NEARER THAN TOWEL?

YES → RUSH BACK TO SEA → SWIMMING

NO → GET TOWEL

Project 1

Identikit

Have you seen the identikit pictures used by the police to help to find criminals? They have drawings of eyes, mouths, hair, ears, noses and so on. To make a face, you pick out the bits you want and fit them together.

Imagine the funny faces you could make.

You could do the same with a computer. You can make up a lot of different parts of faces using all the graphics characters, keyboard letters and symbols.

We have made up simple faces (opposite), but *you* could make them quite detailed. It is even possible to let the computer select the parts at random (using RND) and then print many different faces.

What about drawing your own face this way? Try it — if you dare!

```
 20 CLS : PRINT : PRINT : PRINT
 40 FOR i=1 TO 15
 50 PRINT "   ▌";TAB 16;"▌"
 60 NEXT i
 70 GO SUB 100: GO TO 70
 90 REM *********************
100 LET h$="*!*!*!**!*!*!*"
110 PRINT AT 3,3;h$
120 LET r$="▄▄": LET l$="▙▄ "
130 PRINT AT 5,6;r$;TAB 11;l$
140 INK 2: PRINT AT 0,0;"Which
eyes? (1-3)": INK 0
150 IF INKEY$<>"" THEN GO TO 15
0
160 LET c$=INKEY$: IF c$="" THE
N GO TO 160
170 IF c$="1" THEN LET l$="▪  "
: LET r$=l$
180 IF c$="2" THEN LET l$=" _ "
: LET r$=" _ "
190 IF c$="3" THEN LET l$="  ▪"
: LET r$="▪  "
200 PRINT AT 7,6;r$;TAB 11;l$
210 LET n$=" ▟ ": PRINT AT 11,
8;n$
220 INK 1: PRINT AT 0,0;"Which
mouth? (1-2)": INK 0
230 IF INKEY$<>"" THEN GO TO 23
0
240 LET c$=INKEY$: IF c$="" THE
N GO TO 240
250 IF c$="1" THEN LET m$="▜
 ▄▟"
260 IF c$="2" THEN LET m$="  ▙
▄ "
270 PRINT AT 14,6;m$
280 LET c$="▄▄▄▄▄▄▄▄▄"
290 PRINT AT 18,3;c$
300 RETURN
```

```
  20 MODE 7
  25 PRINT''''
  30 FOR I = 6 TO 19
  40 PRINT CHR$151 SPC5 CHR$234 SPC16 C
HR$53
  50 NEXT
  60 PROCgetfeatures
  70 PRINT'
 110 PRINT TAB(14,12) nose$
 140 GOTO60
 150 REM*******************
 160 DEF PROCgetfeatures
 170 hair$=STRING$(9,"*!")
 175 PRINT TAB(6,5) hair$
 180 rbrow$="p,,":lbrow$=",,p"
 185 PRINTTAB(10,7) rbrow$ SPC4 lbrow$
 190 PRINT TAB(1,3)CHR$129"What type of
eyes? (1-3)"
 200 ch$=GET$
 210 IF ch$="1" reye$="!  ":leye$="!  "
 220 IF ch$="2" reye$=" p ":leye$=" p "
 230 IF ch$="3" reye$="  "+CHR$255:leye
$=CHR$255+"  "
 235 PRINT TAB(10,9)reye$ SPC4 leye$
 240 nose$=".-"
 245 PRINT TAB(14,12) nose$
 246 PRINT TAB(1,3)CHR$132"What type of
mouth? (1-2)":ch$=GET$
 250 IF ch$="1" mouth$="  ''''''''+"
 255 IF ch$="2" mouth$="    tx   "
 256 PRINT TAB(9,15) mouth$
 260 chin$="t,,,,,,   ,,,,,,%"
 265 PRINT TAB(6,19) chin$
 270 ENDPROC
```

Project 2

Disco dazzle

An important part of discos and rock concerts is the lighting. Computers are used to control the special effects. TV pop shows use computers to create interesting images.

Even with a small computer it is possible to create dazzling displays to fit your favourite pop song.

To be most effective you need colour and movement. We can't do this in a book but these descriptions may give you an idea.

1 Different coloured flashing stripes.

```
20 CLS
30 LET col=INT (RND*8)
40 INK col
50 PRINT "████████████
████████"
60 POKE 23692,255
70 PAUSE 15
80 GO TO 30
```

```
20 CLS
30 colour = RND(7)+144
40 PRINT CHR$(colour);
50 FOR I = 1 TO 39
60 PRINT CHR$(255);
70 NEXT
80 GOTO 30
```

2 Any shape repeated randomly around the screen.

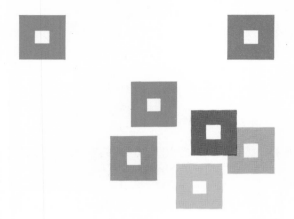

3 Repeat a shape to make a regular pattern.

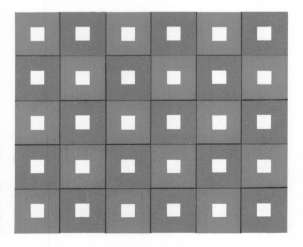

4 Move letters or graphics characters around the screen with steady movement.

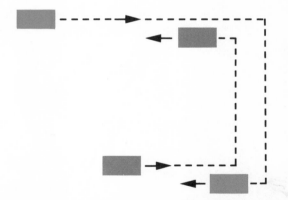

Remember that you should use pauses in the display to make the effects match the rhythm of the music. The short program on page 10 shows you one way of making a pause.

Project 3

Story box

You can tell a story by using a series of picture boxes or frames.

The same can be done using a computer.

First you need to work out your story as a series of frames. The frames can include movement and sound effects as well as the picture. You draw the pictures on squared paper so that they can be turned into computer pictures like the big duck on page 7. When you've finished you can view the story by pressing a key to 'turn over' the pages.

I wish
I wasn't an ugly duckling

I'll hide in these reeds

Six months later . . .

I'm a SWAN!! Yippeee!

Here are some other ideas:

1. Nursery rhymes
(eg Hickory Dickory Dock)
2. A conjuror taking a rabbit from a hat.
3. An acorn grows into a tree.

Don't forget that you can use sound with your story. The program below shows a rocket taking off after a countdown.

```
20 CLS
30 INK 3
40 PRINT AT 20,16;"▄▙▄"
42 POKE 23692,255
45 INK 1
50 FOR I=1 TO 5
60 PRINT TAB 16;"███"
70 NEXT I
80 PRINT TAB 15;"▟████▙"
100 FOR I=5 TO 1 STEP -1
110 PRINT AT 0,23-3*I;"  ";I
120 BEEP 0.2,17: PAUSE 20
130 NEXT I
135 INK 2
140 PRINT AT 21,0: PRINT TAB 15
;"*!*!*"
150 FOR I=1 TO 22
160 PRINT : PAUSE 3
170 NEXT I
180 INK 0
```

```
20 MODE 7
30 PRINT TAB(17,23)CHR$149 CHR$120 CH
R$255 CHR$116
40 FOR I=1 TO 5
50 PRINT CHR$151 SPC17 CHR$255 CHR$25
5CHR$255
60 NEXT
70 PRINT CHR$147 SPC16 CHR$120 CHR$25
5CHR$255 CHR$255 CHR$116
80 FOR count=5 TO 1 STEP -1
90 VDU7
100 PRINT TAB(20-3*count,0)count"   "
110 FOR J=1 TO 1500:NEXT
120 NEXT
130 PRINT TAB(15,24) CHR$129 CHR$136 "
*!*!*"
140 FOR I = 1 TO 24
150 PRINT
160 FOR J = 1 TO 300:NEXT
170 NEXT
```

Rescue station

Type this program and RUN it:

```
 20 PRINT "Press a letter for t
he morse    code.": PRINT
 30 LET c$=INKEY$
 40 IF c$="" THEN GO TO 30
 50 PRINT c$;" ";
 60 IF c$="s" THEN PRINT ". . .
": GO SUB 100: GO SUB 100: GO SU
B 100
 70 IF c$="o" THEN PRINT "_ _ _
": GO SUB 200: GO SUB 200: GO SU
B 200
 80 GO TO 30
 90 REM sound of dot
100 BEEP .1,3
110 FOR J=1 TO 10: NEXT J
120 RETURN
200 REM sound of dash
210 BEEP .3,3
220 FOR K=1 TO 10: NEXT K
230 RETURN
```

… _ _ _ … S O S … _ _ _ …

People all over the world use this code to call for help.

Imagine you are in charge of a rescue station and you hear the SOS code.

You know it means *Save Our Souls*!

How do people learn Morse code? They could use a computer!

```
   20 CLS:PRINT''''"Press a key for morse
code"
   30 ch$=GET$:PRINTch$"    ";
   40 IF ch$="S" THEN PRINT". . .":PROCd
ot:PROCdot:PROCdot
   50 IF ch$ = "O" THEN  PRINT"- - -":PR
OCdash:PROCdash:PROCdash
   60   GOTO 30
   70 REM********************
   80 DEF PROCdot
   90 SOUND1,-10,400,1
  100 FOR I = 1 TO 400:NEXT
  110 ENDPROC
  120 REM*********************
  130 DEF PROCdash
  140 SOUND1,-10,400,6
  150 FOR I = 1 TO 600:NEXT
  160 ENDPROC
```

Now type SOS and see what happens.

This program can be changed to show all the alphabet in Morse code. Can you think how to do it?

A	• –		N	– •
B	– • • •		O	– – –
C	– • – •		P	• – – •
D	– • •		Q	– – • –
E	•		R	• – •
F	• • – •		S	• • •
G	– – •		T	–
H	• • • •		U	• • –
I	• •		V	• • • –
J	• – – –		W	• – –
K	– • –		X	– • • –
L	• – • •		Y	– • – –
M	– –		Z	– – • •

You could learn the code using your program and this list.

Why not make up your own *secret* code? You would have one program to make the coded message which is then de-coded by your friend using another program.

Project 5

Computer snap

Computer snap? You think it sounds too easy? Not likely! Here's an electronic version that can be a real test of skills. As with the card game Snap! you need a good eye, quick thinking and fast reactions to win. The computer can also be programmed to catch out cheats!

Look carefully at these sets of words:

If you saw these sets of words one after the other, which would you say, 'Snap!' to?

It depends on what rules you chose. If your rule for a correct 'snap' was that both the word and the colour have to be the same, then set 3 is the only true snap.

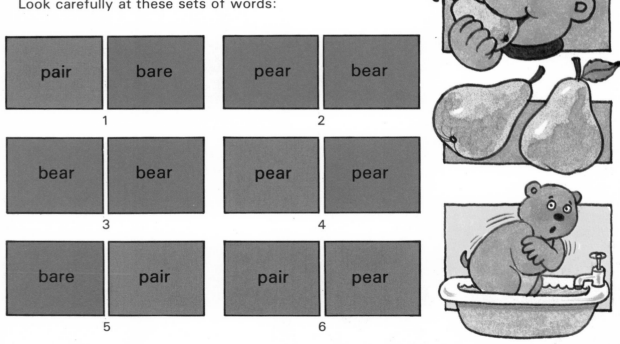

pair	bare
1	

pear	bear
2	

bear	bear
3	

pear	pear
4	

bare	pair
5	

pair	pear
6	

```
  10 REM Snap- Use z,m to play
  20 LET s1=0: LET s2=0
  30 CLS: INK 0
  40 PRINT AT 19,10;s1;AT 19,22;
s2
  50 LET c1=INT (RND*2+1): GO SU
B 1000
  60 LET a$=t$
  70 LET c2=INT (RND*2+1): GO SU
B 1000
  80 LET b$=t$
 85 INK c1
  90 PRINT AT INT (RND*17),INT (
RND*14);a$
  95 INK c2
  97 PRINT AT INT (RND*19),14+IN
T (RND*14);b$
 100 LET t=0
 110 LET t=t+1: LET c$=INKEY$
 120 IF c$="" AND t<70 THEN GO T
O 110
 130 IF c$="" AND a$=b$ AND c1=c
2 THEN BEEP 0.2,-10
 140 IF c$="m" AND a$=b$ AND c1=
c2 THEN LET s2=s2+1: BEEP 0.2,30
 150 IF c$="z" AND a$=b$ AND c1=
c2 THEN LET s1=s1+1: BEEP 0.2,20
 160 IF c$<>"" AND (a$<>b$ OR c1
<>c2) THEN BEEP 0.2,-20
 170 GO TO 30
1000 REM returns a rand string
1010 LET x=INT (RND*4)+1
1020 IF x=1 THEN LET t$="bear"
1030 IF x=2 THEN LET t$="bare"
1040 IF x=3 THEN LET t$="pair"
1050 IF x=4 THEN LET t$="pear"
1060 RETURN
```

In the computer game, sets of words like these appear. You press one key for a 'snap' — your friend uses another key.

If you are first, your score increases by one. When you both miss a 'snap', the computer 'beeps' to let you know!

```
  10 REM Snap - use Z and /
  15 scoreA=0:scoreB=0
  20 MODE7
  25 PRINT TAB(0,21)scoreA;SPC10,scoreB
  30 s1$=CHR$(RND(2)+128)+FNrandstring
  40 s2$=CHR$(RND(2)+128)+FNrandstring
  50 PRINT TAB(RND(14),RND(20))s1$TAB(2
0+RND(14),RND(20))s2$
  60 ch$=INKEY$(100)
  70 IF ch$="" AND s1$=s2$ THEN SOUND0,
-15,9,3
  80 IF ch$="/" AND s1$=s2$ THEN scoreB
=scoreB+1
  90 IF ch$="Z" AND s1$=s2$ THEN scoreA
=scoreA+1
 110 IF ch$<>"" AND s1$<>s2$ THEN SOUND
0,-15,18,6
 120 GOTO20
 130 REM*****************
 140 REM Returns a random string
 150 DEF FNrandstring
 160 ON RND(4) GOTO 170,180,190,200
 170 ="bear"
 180 ="bare"
 190 ="pair"
 200 ="pear"
```

There are many ideas you could include to improve this game.

1 If you press for 'snap' when it isn't, your opponent gets an extra point.
2 Players' names are entered and the first one to score five is the winner and gets a fanfare.
3 You can invent your own rules or use different words or pictures. Which of these would you say is 'snap'?
4 You can have different levels of difficulty by changing the time you see the words and the time you have for pressing a key for 'snap'.
5 Games for a single player could test reaction times by seeing how quickly you can press for a 'snap'.

Happy snapping!

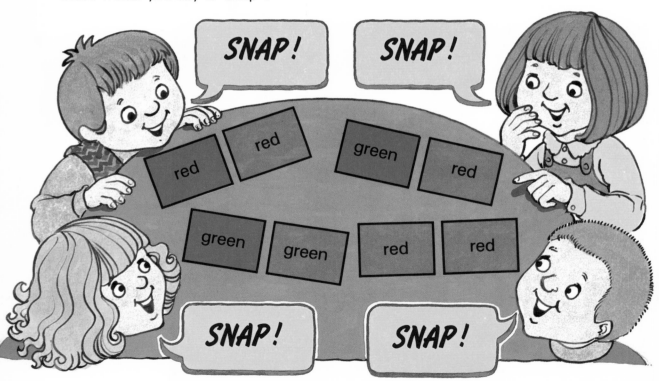

Project 6

Silly keyboard

Suppose that you tell your friends that you have a new program for them to try. It says on the screen, 'Please type your name.' When they try to type their name the letters come out all wrong! No matter how hard they try it still looks silly!

Here's a short program to start you off:

```
20 CLS
30 PRINT''''"Please type your name."''
40 ch$ = GET$
50 PRINT CHR$(RND(126)+128);
60 GOTO 40
70 NEXT
80 GOTO 30
```

```
20 CLS
30 PRINT : PRINT : PRINT : PRI
NT
40 PRINT "Please type your nam
e."
50 LET c$=INKEY$
60 IF c$="" THEN GO TO 50
70 INK INT (RND*8)
80 PRINT CHR$ (INT (RND*132)+3
2);
90 GO TO 50
```

You could make the computer do some extra things.

Suppose after a short time it started making noises and the message changed to 'Stop messing about...TYPE YOUR NAME PROPERLY!'

You could even make it look as though the computer didn't want to be used! Messages like, 'Ouch!', 'Stop it!', 'Leave me alone!' could appear as your friend types.

Project 7
Star search

Here's the beginning of a game you can play with lots of further ideas for making your own super version. Type in the program and RUN it. The object is to find things which are hidden in a square which is five boxes wide and five boxes high.

```
 10 CLS : LET D$="
                   ": REM 32 spa
ces for deleting a line
 20 REM Print out array
 30 INPUT AT 5,0;"How many hidd
en things";Maximum
 40 LET Hits=0: LET Finish=0
 50 DIM G$(5,5)
 60 DIM H$(5,5)
 70 GO SUB 480: REM Load array
 80 GO SUB 270: REM Hide things
 90 GO SUB 200: REM Print array
100 REM Main loop
105 POKE 23674,0: POKE 23673,0:
POKE 23672,0
110 PRINT AT 15,0;"Make a guess
:";TAB (18);AT 17,0;TAB (20);AT
18,0;TAB (20)
113 LET Time=INT ((65536*PEEK 2
3674+256*PEEK 23673+PEEK 23672)/
50)
115 PRINT AT 10,16;Time;" secon
ds"
120 INPUT "Across :";Guess1
130 INPUT " Down :";Guess2
135 IF Guess1=0 THEN STOP
140 IF Guess1>5 OR Guess2>5 OR
Guess1<1 OR Guess2<1 THEN GO TO
110
150 IF H$(Guess2,guess1)="*" TH
EN GO SUB 400: GO TO 180
160 PRINT AT 15,0;TAB 32;AT 15,
0;"Sorry you missed... Try again
.": BEEP .5,-3: BEEP .5,-5
165 PRINT AT 15,0;D$
170 GO SUB 330
180 IF Finish=0 THEN GO TO 110
190 CLS : STOP
200 REM Print out array
210 CLS
220 FOR D=1 TO 5
230 PRINT AT 5+D,5;G$(D)
240 NEXT D
250 RETURN
270 REM Put items in to find
280 FOR L=1 TO Maximum
290 LET Pos1=INT (RND)*5+1: LET
Pos2=INT (RND*5)+1
300 LET H$(Pos1,Pos2)="*"
310 NEXT L
320 RETURN
330 REM Space bar press
340 PRINT AT 20,0;"Press the SP
ACE KEY to continue."
350 IF INKEY$<>" " THEN GO TO 3
50
370 PRINT AT 20,0;D$
380 RETURN
390 REM Hit routine
400 PRINT AT 18,25;"A HIT!"
410 LET Hits=Hits+1
420 FOR L=1 TO 4: BEEP .5,4: BE
EP .5,7: NEXT L
430 IF Hits>=Maximum THEN CLS :
PRINT AT 12,0;"You've hit them
all";AT 14,0;"Well done!": LET F
inish=1: GO SUB 330: RETURN
440 PAUSE 3
450 LET G$(Guess2,Guess1)="*"
460 GO SUB 200: REM Print new a
rray
470 RETURN
480 REM Load array with "?"
490 FOR D=1 TO 5
500 LET G$(D)="?????"
510 NEXT D
520 RETURN
```

```
  10 CLS
  20 REM Set up game
  30 INPUTTAB(0,5)"How many hidden thin
gs?"Maximum
  40 Hits=0:Finish=0
  50 DIMGame$(5,5)
  60 DIMHide$(5,5)
  70 GOSUB500:REM Load array
  80 GOSUB290:REM Hide objects
  90 GOSUB220:REM Print array
 100 REM Main loop
 110 TIME=0
 120 PRINTTAB(0,15)"Make a guess :";SPC
(18);TAB(0,17)SPC(20);TAB(0,18)SPC(20)
 130 PRINTTAB(16,15)(TIME DIV 100)DIV 6
0;" Mins ";(TIME DIV 100)MOD 60;" Secs"
 140 INPUTTAB(0,17)"Across : "Guess1
 150 INPUTTAB(0,18)"Down   : "Guess2
 160 IFGuess1>5 OR Guess1<1 OR Guess2>5
OR Guess2<1 THEN 120
 170  IF Hide$(Guess1,Guess2)="*" THEN
GOSUB 420:GOTO200
 180 PRINTTAB(0,15);SPC(40);TAB(0,15)"S
orry you missed... Try again.":SOUND1,-1
5,53,10:SOUND1,-15,23,10
 190 GOSUB350
 200 IF Finish=0 THEN GOTO120
 210 CLS:END
 220 REM Print out array
 230 CLS
 240 FOR Down=1 TO 5
 250   FOR Across=1 TO 5
 260     PRINTTAB(11+Across,5+Down)Game
$(Across,Down);
 270     NEXTAcross:NEXTDown

 280 RETURN
 290 REM Put in items to find
 300 FOR Loop= 1 TO Maximum
 310   Pos1=RND(5):Pos2=RND(5)
 320   Hide$(Pos1,Pos2)="*"
 330   NEXT Loop
 340 RETURN
 350 REM Space bar press
 360 PRINTTAB(0,20)"Press space bar to
continue."
 370 OK$=GET$
 380 IFOK$<>" "THEN370
 390 PRINTTAB(0,20)SPC(38)
 400 RETURN
 410 REM Hit routine
 420 PRINT TAB(25,18)"A HIT!"
 430 Hits=Hits+1
 440 FORLoop=1TO4:SOUND1,-15,53,5:SOUND
1,-15,89,5:NEXT
 450 IF Hits>=Maximum THEN CLS: PRINTTA
B(0,12)"You've found them all!";'';"Well
Done!";'';"You took ";(TIME DIV 100)DIV
60;" Mins ";(TIME DIV 100)MOD 60;" Secs
.":Finish=1:GOSUB350:RETURN
 460 FOR Pause=1 TO 2000:NEXT
 470 Game$(Guess1,Guess2)="*"
 480 GOSUB220:REM Print new array
 490 RETURN
 500 REM Load array with '?'
 510 FOR Across=1TO5
 520   FOR Down=1TO5
 530     Game$(Across,Down)="?"
 540     NEXT Down:NEXT Across
 550 RETURN
```

To play, answer the first question and then the screen will look like this:

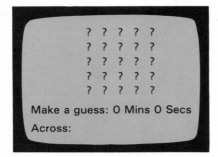

CAN YOU FIND THE STARS ?

Type the number of the column (across) that you think contains a hidden star. Press RETURN. Do the same for the row (down).

If you don't find a star you press the SPACE BAR (ENTER on the Spectrum) to try again and the computer tells you how long you've been looking.

If you find a star, you're told and the one you found is printed in the correct position. When you've found all the stars the program gives you a final time.

As a diagram the program looks like this:

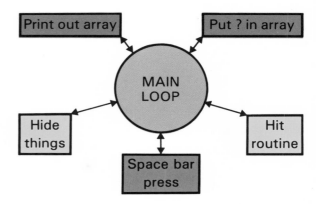

Look at the program listing to see how it works. Notice that the program is divided into sections like this:

Lines
10 to 90	– Getting everything
10 to 90	ready to start
100 to 210	– The main loop of
100 to 200	the program
210 to 520	– The sections or
220 to 550	– subroutines that

Sinclair in red   do particular jobs

Each group of lines has a job to do. The main (loop) part of the program calls each routine as it is needed. On the BBC micro the subroutines could be procedures instead.

Writing and organising your program like this makes it much easier to find errors and see how it is supposed to work. The fun really starts when you add sections to make your own program.

Here are some suggestions:

1 A routine to give clues as to where things are hidden.
   eg 'warm', 'cold'

2 A routine to show where you've already looked.

3 A routine to give better sound effects at each stage.

Other things you could do to improve the program are:

1 Allow the player to change the size of the square.
   eg to ten by ten.

2 Turn off the auto-repeat and cursor (see pages 31 and 32).

3 Keep a check on which objects have been found so that each one only counts once.

4 Add a score page and title (see page 30).

5 Think up a reason for the game.
   eg You are trying to find gold in a maze; you are hunting creatures in a jungle; you are looking for a magic word.

If you like, you could hide two or three different items in the square. The program does different things when the items are found. For example, suppose the players were looking for treasure. Some boxes in the square might contain treasure, some might have man-eating tigers.

Go on...type in the program and think of some more ideas to improve your game program.

Polishing up your programs

Each project in this book has suggestions for adding extra things so that the program becomes your own. One of the best ways to learn about programming your computer is to copy a short program and then experiment.

First RUN the program to see what happens.

Then work out what instructions the computer follows and decide what changes or additions you want to make. Your changes may be different colours or extra sounds; the number of times something happens; you may want to slow things down or speed them up; add a score or a program title or a new section you hadn't thought of before.

While you are improving your program, you may find that it no longer works. Don't panic! Every programmer finds that this happens. Indeed you are lucky to get a program to RUN first time! It's more likely that you will find it has errors or 'bugs' that need to be found and removed.

Part of the fun of programming is discovering and removing these bugs. It's like a detective game — and the computer will help you by giving error messages (on the BBC) or reports (on the Spectrum).

For example:

Spectrum
Variable not found *(line number)*
(The Spectrum manual has information about the error reports.)

BBC
Syntax error at *(line number)*
(BBC *User Guide* has information about the error messages.)

Don't try to read all of your computer manual in one go! Use the index; dip into it to find the clues and information you need to solve a problem.

Very small things, like a missing comma or an extra space, can be enough to prevent your program RUNning. Corrections can be made by re-typing the whole line correctly or by editing the faulty line. (Details about how to edit listings can be found in your manual.)

Easy mistakes to avoid

CHECK FOR THE COMMON MISTAKES FIRST!

Here are some suggestions as to how they may have happened

1 *A line is missing.* You probably forgot to give it a line number!

2 *Two lines are all in one.* You didn't press RETURN or ENTER at the end of the first line!

3 *An incorrect figure or symbol has been used.* Many are easily confused. For example:
letter O and 0 (zero)
( ) and [ ]
$ (string sign) and S

Some confusion arises because BASIC looks a lot like written English. However, BASIC follows its own rules as the next two common mistakes suggest.

4 *Spaces are missing, in the wrong place or there are too many of them.*

5 *Punctuation marks of all kinds eg ; : , . ( ) '' '' can be missed or misplaced.* In BASIC they certainly are used very differently, so be careful!

6 *Too many things: extra words, spaces and punctuation marks have appeared.* Probably you held your finger on a key for too long and the 'auto-repeat' caused those extra things to be printed.

7 *Command words (eg THEN, CHR$, NEXT) were not properly entered.*

Spectrum Take great care that you have the machine in the correct Mode (K, L, C, E or G) and enter the command by a single key press, rather than trying to type the word letter by letter. (See your manual.) The modes are:
K keywords   E extended
L letters   C capitals
G graphics (It's easy to forget to change back after typing graphic symbols.)

Extras for your programs

Here are some ideas that you might use to improve your programs, making them look more polished and professional.

Title pages

Have you noticed that when you load some programs from cassette, a title page appears first and this remains while the rest of the program is loading? You might like to design a title page.

You could invent a personal design or badge that could be used for all your programs, changing the program name each time. Or each program could have its own special title page design.

Whatever you choose to do, you will have two programs — the Title (or Header) program is followed by the Main program on your cassette tape.

Let's say that you have written a program and now want to add a title page. This is what you might do.

1 Design your title page and write the program.

2 Include at the end of this program some code that tells the computer to LOAD the main program and then RUN it.

3 SAVE this title program. (For Spectrum users this is not the usual kind of program SAVE. Look at the code below.)

4 Now SAVE your main program on the very next section of the cassette tape.

5 Rewind your tape and LOAD the program to check that the title page loads and stays on the screen while the main program is loading.

Here's one example of code you can have at the end of your title program.

Spectrum

Example title program
```
10 PRINT AT 10,0; "Please wait. The main program is loading."
20 INK 1:PAPER 7:REM (so that you cannot see what the Spectrum writes)
30 LOAD"Main":REM (this loads the next part)
```

You must SAVE this title program using
SAVE"*filename*"LINE 10
(Line 10 tells the computer to GOTO line
10 as soon as it has finished LOADing.)

When you SAVE the main program on
the next section of the cassette, you
must use this instruction:
SAVE "Main" LINE 10
(Our example is LINE 10; yours may well
have another line number. Details of this
can be found in the Spectrum manual.)

BBC

Example title program
30 PRINT TAB(0,10) "Please wait. The
main program is loading."
20 CHAIN *"filename of main
program"*:REM (*this loads the next part*)

Useful things to know

Why not start a notebook? Most
computer programmers have one to write
down useful ideas.

Here are some ideas to start you off.

Spectrum

1 To stop the computer asking
   'scroll?', include this statement.
   POKE23692,255 (see manual).
   This can be useful when you want to
   have some kinds of moving graphics
   such as a rocket rising up the screen.

2 Use POKE23561,255 to (almost)
   remove the auto repeat effect when
   pressing keys.

3 To get the computer to wait for any
   key to be pressed before continuing,
   include a line using INKEY$.

   For example:
   150 PRINT AT 20,3;"Press any key to
   continue."
   160 IF INKEY$ = "" THEN GOTO 160
   (This example was at line 160. Use
   whatever line number you are at in
   your program but remember to use
   that same number after GOTO.)

4 If you want to check on a yes or no
   (Y/N) answer, there's a routine over
   the page that will do this.
   There are lots of uses for this routine.
   Our example is for asking if you wish
   to play another game.

The main part of your program...

```
480 PRINT "Do you want to play again?
(Y/N)"
490 GOSUB 1000
500 IF yes THEN GOTO 10:REM (takes you
back to the start of the program)
510 STOP
```

```
1000 LET C$=INKEY$
1010 IF C$="Y" OR C$="y" THEN LET
yes=1
1020 IF C$="N" OR C$="n" THEN LET
yes=0
1030 IF C$="y" OR C$="Y" OR C$="n"
OR C$="N" THEN RETURN
1040 GOTO 1000
```

BBC

1 To turn the flashing cursor off, include this statement in your program.

    VDU23;8202;0;0;0;

Use a MODE statement (*eg* MODE 7) to turn it back on.

2 The command ✻FX11,0 turns off the auto repeat altogether. ✻FX12 turns it back on. (See the *User Guide*.)

3 Use ✻FX210,1 to turn off sound. Use ✻FX210,0 to turn sound back on.

4 Use ✻FX220 to turn off ESCAPE. Switch it back on using ✻FX220,27

5 To stop your program from being lost if BREAK is pressed, put this at the beginning of your program:

    ✻KEY10 OLD¦M RUN¦M

If you leave out the RUN¦M, the program will not be lost. You just have to type RUN yourself!
(The sign ¦ is one of those next to the arrow keys. See your *User Guide*.)

6 If you want to check on a yes or no (Y/N) answer, the routine below will do this. There are lots of uses for this routine. Our example is asking if you wish to play another game.

The main part of your program...

```
350 PRINT "Do you want to play again?
(Y/N)"
360 ;IF FNyesno THEN RUN
370 ;END
```

```
1000 DEF FNyesno
1010 LOCALch$
1020 ch$=GET$
1030 IF INSTR("ynYN",ch$)=0 THEN 1020
1040 =(INSTR("yY",ch$)<>0)
```